EXPLORE THE WORLD

SOCIAL SCIENCE

A World of Spies

ELLEN LEWIS

TABLE OF CONTENTS

The World of Spies	2
What Is a Spy?	6
Spies in History	10
What Kind of Spy Are You?	16
Glossary/Index	20

PIONEER VALLEY EDUCATIONAL PRESS, INC

THE WORLD OF SPIES

Take a look around you. What do you see?

Is that pen just an ordinary pen?
Or is it filled with invisible ink?
Maybe it was used to send a **coded** letter
to someone on the other side of the world.

Is that rock over there really a rock?
Or does it have a hidden **compartment**?
Maybe there's a piece of **evidence**
or a key to a secret building
tucked somewhere inside it.

Is that coat just a regular raincoat? Or could its buttons hold a tiny camera? Maybe a switch in the pockets can be clicked to snap pictures of something very far away.

Lipstick pistol

Micro Unmanned Aerial Vehicle (UAV) or "Insectothopter"

Hollow silver dollar

Hidden compass cufflinks

Subminiature radio receiver pipe

Subminiature camera

Unmanned Underwater Vehicle (UUV) Robot fish "Charlie"

Look closely at the world around you. There could be spies anywhere.

WHAT IS A SPY?

A spy is someone who tries to discover secret information.

A lot of information can be found by searching in a library or on the Internet for a few minutes. But some information is kept hidden, and only a few people know about it. A spy is an expert at getting this kind of information without being found out.

Some spies work for their country. Other spies sell information for money. All spies have to work secretly so that other people will not catch them.

In the past, spies used simple tools, such as safety pins, invisible ink, and hollow coins. Today, spies use all kinds of amazing **gadgets**.

Tiny cameras can be hidden inside a pair of sunglasses. A microphone can be placed inside a watch. There is even a special X-ray liquid that allows you to see the mail inside an envelope without opening it.

MORE TO EXPLORE

The **INTERNATIONAL SPY MUSEUM** is located in Washington, DC. At the museum, you can try out actual spy gadgets, view secret documents, and learn about the history of spying.

To become a spy, you have to learn many skills.

One of the most important spy skills is **observation**. A spy is a close observer of the objects and people nearby.

Spies also have to analyze the information they gather, wear **disguises**, and learn to sneak in and out of places without being caught.

Even kids can be spies! A 14-year-old boy carried coded messages inside the **BUTTONS** of his coat to his brother, who was a soldier during the Revolutionary War. The buttons hid secret messages for George Washington!

MORE TO EXPLORE

9

SPIES IN HISTORY

What do George Washington, Benjamin Franklin, and Harriet Tubman have in common? They were all spies!

George Washington is famous for being the first president of the United States. But did you know that he was also a spy? During the Revolutionary War, he created an organization called the Culper Spy Ring. Spies in the Culper Spy Ring risked their lives to get information about the British army and pass it back to Washington.

MORE TO EXPLORE

One of the **CULPER SPIES** was a housewife. She hung clothes on her clothesline in patterns to send signals to George Washington. Her neighbors thought she was just doing her laundry!

11

Benjamin Franklin was a famous inventor. He was also a spy. His work as a spy convinced the French government to support America during the Revolutionary War.

Harriet Tubman is famous for being a "conductor" on the Underground Railroad. She guided slaves who were escaping the South and hoping to gain their freedom in the North. She was also a spy.

During the Civil War, Tubman worked for the Union Army as a nurse and a cook— and as a spy. She could disguise herself as a slave, so no one would pay attention to her. That allowed her to move easily among enemy camps. They never suspected her activities.

Not all spies are people. Pigeons were often used as spies during wars. They were sent across the ocean to deliver coded messages and instructions back and forth between different countries. Sometimes they even carried little cameras that would take photos of enemy camps.

A pigeon named Cher Ami ("Dear Friend") was one of the most famous spies of World War I. She was sent by a group of American soldiers with a small can tied to her. The soldiers hid a message inside the can.

Cher Ami was badly hurt during her flight. She was blinded in one eye and lost one of her legs, but she still arrived at the American headquarters. By delivering that secret message, Cher Ami saved the lives of almost 200 American soldiers.

>> Many pigeons were honored as war heroes. They received medals for their brave service.

WHAT KIND OF SPY ARE YOU?

At the International Spy Museum in Washington, DC, you will learn about four kinds of spies: ninja, cloak, shadow, and dagger.

Can you secretly enter enemy **territory**, find the information you need, and leave without being caught? If so, you may be a perfect ninja spy.

Ninja spies are mysterious. They can get in and out of buildings secretly without being seen. They gather information from places and then seem to disappear like magic.

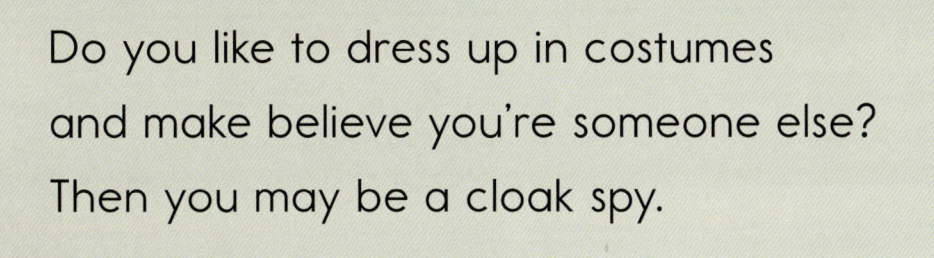

Do you like to dress up in costumes and make believe you're someone else? Then you may be a cloak spy.

Cloak spies are masters of disguise. They can make themselves into different people in a matter of seconds. They use mustaches, makeup, costumes, languages, and wigs. They pretend to have different jobs so they can go unnoticed.

Do you like secret messages and puzzles? Could you find a way to send messages using invisible ink and secret codes? You may like being a shadow spy.

Shadow spies can also break other people's codes and read secret messages.

The most frequently used letters in the alphabet are *e, t, a, o, i,* and *n*. A **SHADOW SPY** can use this information to break a code. Look for the most common letters in a coded message, replace them with any of these six letters, and see if that reveals part of a word.

k̄ d̄f̄k̄ḡp̄ē d̄c̄ā m̄d̄ k̄ d̄v̄k̄x̄h̄ k̄ȳḡ j̄ōw̄t̄w̄x̄ c̄w̄x̄d̄p̄ȳ.

Answer: A shadow spy is a smart and clever person.

Do you like action?
Can you imagine planning
a daring rescue mission?
You may be a good dagger spy.

Dagger spies work in dangerous settings. They plant **electronic** devices in hidden places or use tunnels to escape being captured. They may be asked to rescue someone.

Secret Compartments

Spies use everyday items to hide secret messages. Rocks, books, and food jars can all hide secret compartments. Hollow coins, books, and the heels of shoes are good hiding places too.

Secret Writing

Secret messages can be sent in different ways. Some spies use invisible ink. Some use codes or ciphers made of numbers and letters.

Shoes

Spies may hide microphones and other devices in the heels of their shoes. Sometimes they plant these devices in their enemies' shoes!

Secret Messages

Eat your words! Some spies eat their messages after reading them. Secret writing paper can be made from potato, sugar, and vanilla. Read the message and then swallow the evidence!

Spy Tools

Spies use special equipment to carry out their missions. The International Spy Museum has many spy tools and artifacts on display.

Wristwatch
Watches with cameras and listening devices are excellent tools for spies.

Buttonhole Camera
Spies often use coats with camera buttons. The fake buttons have little lenses. The spy will keep one hand in their pocket to click a device that takes the picture.

Disguise Kits
Disguises are very important spy tools. A disguise kit may contain hair, clothes, makeup, and even a false nose for a spy to wear to quickly become someone else.

GLOSSARY

coded
using a set of letters, numbers, or symbols to hide the meaning of a message

compartment
an enclosed storage space inside something larger

disguises
changes in appearance that hide a person's true identity

electronic
a device that uses electricity

evidence
an object or observation that shows something to be factual

gadgets
small devices designed to perform a task or solve a problem

observation
paying close attention to the world around you

territory
an area of land owned by a government

INDEX

Benjamin Franklin 10, 12
buttons 4, 8
camera 4, 7, 14
captured 8, 16, 19
Cher Ami 15
Civil War 13
cloak 16-17
coded 2, 8, 14, 18
compartment 3
costumes 17
Culper Spy Ring 10
dagger 16, 19
disguises 8, 13, 17
electronic 19
evidence 3
gadgets 7
George Washington 8, 10
information 6, 8, 10, 16, 18
International Spy Museum 7, 16
invisible ink 2, 7, 18
Harriet Tubman 10, 13
languages 17
makeup 17
ninja 16
observation 8
pen 2
pigeons 14-15
rescue 19
Revolutionary War 8, 10, 12
secret 3, 6, 7, 8, 15, 16, 18
shadow 16, 18
sunglasses 7
territory 16
Underground Railroad 13
wigs 17
World War I 15
X-ray 7